Here's wh
about 7
Your Lif

"Just like your computer has an IP (Identity-Purpose), every Christian has an IP address. Identity is who you are. Purpose is what you do and why you do it. In other words, you are the way you are because of why you are. Simply said, the discovery of your purpose is the discovery of your life. Purpose is what was in God's mind when He created you. Ignorance of purpose does not cancel purpose. The purposes of God stand. Most live for presentation. God designed us to live for purpose.

7 Keys to Unlocking Your Life P.U.R.P.O.S.E. brings illumination giving revelation, thus transformation on the crucial subject of purpose. It is strong where most books on purpose aren't. It gives the 'how to' of purpose. It's strong on implementation and execution. It moves you from the prophetic revelation of purpose to the apostolic reality of purpose. It moves you from dream to done.

In today's world, clarity is a rarity. Thank you, Stuart, for bringing clarity...on purpose."

Dr. Ed Delph, *Nationstrategy*
Phoenix, Arizona

"From beginning to end I couldn't put this book by Stuart Simpson down. It is packed full of very insightful, theologically sound and practical truth, designed to clear out uncertainty and pin down who you really are and why you have been put on this earth for such a time as this. This work book will open your eyes and help you see the bigger picture that is uniquely you. So many people - Christians too, seem to drift through life, never realising who they are and what God has uniquely wired them to be and do. Without such a compass, their destinies are blurred; their purpose goes on hold and their full potential never gets released. Sadly they 'die full'! Our graveyards are full of such people.

Whether you are just starting out in life or have been cutting your groove for many years; whether you feel called to be involved in church work or want to know if God wishes you to be a strong witness in your place of work, Stuart's book will help you sharpen that focus. Using a refreshing acronym of the word, 'purpose', he has produced a unique and very comprehensive tool that both Christians and non-Christians will find useful – even transformational. I feel that this work will become required reading for anyone studying to become a more purpose-filled leader or to find out what constitutes their best career-fit, or a more informed parent, or simply to become a better person. Stuart's book will not disappoint. You will love it!"

Martin Allen, *Founding Director of Caleb Ministries (www.caleb.org.uk)*

"A vital topic, explored with clarity and insight. An invaluable read."

Paul McGee, *Sunday Times best-selling author and international speaker*

"Stuart's new book is a welcome and refreshing new entry into the subject of discovering purpose in the world which is becoming more listless and restless, with many just going through the motions. This book combines a healthy balance between theory and practical exercises to help the readers discover their design in order to discover their life purpose. Thought-provoking and life-giving!"

Deepak Mahtani ACMI, FRSA,
Keynote Speaker & Social Philanthropist

"I've only recently got to know Stuart Simpson but it was obvious from our first meeting that we are 'kindred spirits'.

Stuart believes that discovering our God-given purpose is the key to a fulfilled life and so do I. As a trained life coach Stuart says in Chapter 1, "for humans the greatest tragedy in life is not death but life without purpose" and in this easy-to-read book, he shows us how we can align ourselves with the unique purpose God has in mind for each one of us.

I enjoyed Stuart's use of the word PURPOSE and I found his exercises both helpful and insightful. I was particularly delighted to see that he is keen to help us discover what God wants us to do in the wider world and not simply in what can sometimes prove to be a stifling church context. Like Stuart, I am totally committed to the challenge of "empowering people to manifest the kingdom of God with their time, talent and treasure in an intentional, sustained, practical and strategic way."

For these reasons I am very happy to endorse this book in the hope it will encourage many to be both signs and instruments of God's kingdom here on Earth.

Rev Rob James BA BD,
Church and Media Consultant,
Evangelical Alliance, Wales

"This book is concise and clear, packed with practical wisdom and tools to help you find your P.U.R.P.O.S.E."

Roger Allen, *Enabler, Together4Bristol & Finding Purpose*

"I think it's great! It's a good overview/introduction to the basics of discovering your purpose, with some great exercises and further links so readers can go as deep as they like, when they want to unpack a little more.

Good to have someone with a heart for mission providing a resource about life purpose. So much of today's Christian material on this topic focuses on personal fulfilment that it's good to have something that focuses on kingdom fulfilment and global-minded servanthood."

Mike Frith,
Founding Director,
OSCAR Mission Resources

7 KEYS TO UNLOCKING YOUR LIFE P.U.R.P.O.S.E.

7 KEYS TO UNLOCKING YOUR LIFE P.U.R.P.O.S.E.

Discovering Your Destiny by Understanding Your Design

Stuart M. Simpson

7 Keys to Unlocking Your Life P.U.R.P.O.S.E.:
Discovering Your Destiny by Understanding
Your Design
© Copyright Dr Stuart M. Simpson, 2019

Empower Coaching at
www.stuartmsimpson.com

Catalyst Ministries at www.catalystmin.org

ISBN: 9781092557436

Contents

Introduction

*"The person without a purpose
is like a ship without a rudder."
– Thomas Carlyle*

This book is about discovering your life purpose.

Any internet search will demonstrate that this is a subject that many, many people are interested in.

On Google there are a plethora of different ideas and approaches to finding your life purpose, including:

3 unexpected ways...,

    7 strange questions...,
    10 tips to learn...,
    5 steps to finding...,
    10 deep questions...,
    TED talks.

All of them come with the promise of helping you find and discover what your seemingly elusive 'purpose in life' is.

Why Another Book on Life Purpose?

So what is one more book on the subject got to offer that isn't already available? Let me mention two reasons.

One is worldview which is how we view life and the world we live in. I will write a bit more on this in the next chapter but, suffice to say, a person's worldview will be reflected in how they approach the issue of life purpose.

My worldview is Christian theism. I therefore approach life purpose on the basis that there is a Creator and

Designer, and that every person has been designed and created for a specific purpose, within a transcendent higher or divine purpose. The significance of creating your own purpose and destiny is greatly reduced, if it ends at the grave and doesn't contribute to something greater and eternal.

> **The significance of creating your own purpose and destiny is greatly reduced, if it ends at the grave.**

Secondly, within the Christian world, very few churches pay much or any attention to this subject.

I have been in the church world all of my life, in numerous countries, and I haven't come across any that truly empower people to discover their life purpose in the way I outline in this book.

I'm not referring to merely identifying a person's 'spiritual gifts', nor am I referring to helping people volunteer within a church context.

I mean actually facilitating and empowering people to manifest the kingdom of God with their 'time, talent, and treasure' in an intentional, sustained, practical and strategic way.

In a way that pays attention to their design and calling.

And in a way that is not subjected to a faulty paradigm of thinking (the spiritual-secular divide) which is embedded within much of evangelical Christianity today.

How many churches do you know that actually find out and consider the callings of individual members?

How many churches help people discover and identify their unique design and kingdom calling, and then equip and commission them into their spheres of influence?

Leaders may give exhortations from the platform to 'live for Christ's kingdom', but rarely provide the practical means for those listening to do so once they leave the church building, beyond developing spiritual disciplines for use in their private lives.

However, a key role of leaders is to equip and empower others.[1] Instead of the church being a place of equipping, too many leaders try and assimilate people into their ministry, instead of empowering them into the ministry God has for them! What about empowering people during the main part of their lives, Monday to Saturday, when they spend most of their time?

Vocation & Calling

For some people, especially within the church world, life purpose equates to having a vocation or calling in life.

If we're honest, the question of calling does come with some baggage attached to it. It tends to carry with it feelings of pressure, even guilt, or worth, especially if we feel unsure if God has called us and if not, that we're just not as important as some others.

This is especially true if we believe that only those who go to the mission field or engage in church work are 'called'. It therefore has the tendency to involve comparing ourselves with others.

I'm very aware of this because at the age of eighteen I did hear 'God's call' on my life. This was an unexpected encounter at the end of a large Christian gathering. There wasn't any audible voice, just a deep sense on the inside that God was speaking into my life.

All I understood at that time was that my life would involve teaching and travel. It wasn't until years later that I began to understand my calling would involve cross-cultural mission work overseas. As time has gone by, further clarity has become known in terms of coaching and empowering others.

God calls people on an individual basis. For some people it may involve a dramatic encounter with God, such as Saul's "Damascus Road" experience, Isaiah's vision of God on a highly exalted throne, or Moses' "burning bush".[2] However, as much as we may like a supernatural sign from heaven or an angelic visitation in the night, such experiences are *not* the norm.

The Voice of Design

Whether you experience a 'God-encounter' or not, **God has spoken through your design.** He designed you with your purpose in mind. He has therefore already spoken to you about your purpose and calling.

There are things within you that already point you to your purpose. They are clues showing you the way to go.

Jesus told a parable about talents (the word talent comes directly from this parable).[3] Firstly, the king *called* his servants. He then *equipped* them with resources for the task. And then he told them the task and *commissioned* them to bring it to pass. Finally, after a period of time, he returned and asked them to give an account of how they had used what they had been given.

> **God has spoken through your design.**

This book will help you to *hear* your calling or life purpose. It will help you *discover* your design, which as stated previously, is a voice in itself and a clue to your purpose.

Take Time Out

In the busyness of life it can be hard to stop and take some time to look inside and reflect upon what you see, hear, and recollect.

Sometimes we all need to take a self-inventory. It will bring clarity.

Your life matters.

Your work matters.

Your best contribution in this world matters.

I want to help you live out your unique purpose, discover your calling, and know your God-given design.

I will give you 7 keys to unlock your life purpose and help you start living the life you've been designed to live.

But first, let's consider an age-old question.

7 Keys to Unlocking Your Life P.U.R.P.O.S.E.

Chapter 1

What is Life About?

From the beginning of time, mankind has grappled with the universal questions of meaning and purpose.

Why am I here?

What is the meaning of life?

These are key questions that almost every person asks at some point in time.

Nevertheless, many people just don't think about their life purpose.

To them, life just seems to be about studying, working, starting a family, having children, going for a holiday once in a while, retiring, and then dying from sickness or old age.

However, if the truth be told, there is a deep desire within every person to feel loved, useful...even significant.

Living life without a clear sense of purpose is...merely existing.

People may have full bank accounts, but inside they are empty and unfulfilled.

They may have all the material things a person could ever want, but inside a vacuum still exists.

Living life without a clear sense of purpose is...merely existing.

What do YOU want to do with your life?

Everything in life has a purpose.

YOU are designed for purpose.

Your purpose, your abilities, your origins, your personality and outlook on life cannot be separated.

Your God-given design determines how you will function, which is connected to your purpose in life.

Designed for a Purpose

"The two most important days in life are the day you were born and the day you found out why." (Mark Twain)

Behind every design is a purpose.

No inventor or designer ever created something without a purpose in mind.

No-one constructs a building without there being a purpose for it. The purpose determines its design and function.

Modern 'wisdom' dislikes the concepts of design and purpose. It says we simply evolved to what we are now.

> **Design and purpose lie at the heart of all human life and significance.**

A well-known evolutionist stated that 'man is the result of a purposeless and natural process that did not have him in mind.'[4] Evolutionists believe mankind has simply evolved in order to survive.

But design and purpose lie at the heart of all human life and significance.

Purpose in Nature

There is evidence of design in nature and throughout the created order.

Whether we consider the Earth and the Solar System or the truly amazing human eye, there is undeniable evidence of design.

Consider the human brain which is one of the most astonishing, incredibly complex and tremendously powerful creations.

Large areas of the brain are dedicated to processing speech. For the purpose of speech, human beings have a uniquely long throat, agile tongue, fine lips, and precise vocal cords. During communication some one hundred muscles are at work, and the brain is processing information at a tremendous rate. It is the result of a particularly awesome design.

When it comes to recording design specifications, genetic information is all contained within DNA – what scientists call our 'instruction book for life' – and a pinhead of DNA would have a billion times more information capacity than a 4 gigabyte hard drive.

Things that we think don't serve any useful purpose or can be a nuisance, are here for a reason.

Take wasps for instance. Wasps (along with other insect predators such as spiders) are responsible for the maintenance and control of their prey's populations. If they were removed from the system, the result could be a disastrous imbalance, impacting plants and affecting how they reproduce. This in turn would be bad for ants, which eat and disperse seeds, and then the seeds wouldn't be spread.

Wasps also benefit humans by eating a lot of caterpillars and small white larvae that feed on vegetables.

Wasps also play an important role within the ecosystem and maintain a vitally important biological purpose here on planet Earth.[5] We don't want wasps to join us when we're having a picnic, but otherwise, we need wasps!

A key aspect that separates humans from the animal kingdom is that humans are creative, emotional, and spiritual beings.

Humans are capable of a vast array of emotions and can appreciate beauty through sight, sound, smell, touch, and taste.

We are also uniquely capable of rational thought and self-awareness. Unlike animals that respond to instinct, humans make choices and are responsible for the actions that we take.

Unlike the animal world, we have a responsibility to steward the Earth and our environment.[6]

Designed for Relationship

Furthermore, humans are designed to have deep relationships with others and have unique abilities to be creative in many different ways.

Ultimately, we are here because we are loved by a divine Designer and Creator. Our response is to love Him back, to glorify Him and enjoy Him forever.

Monkeys don't think about the meaning of life or consider their life purpose.

But for humans, **the greatest tragedy in life is not death, but life without purpose.**

It can be dangerous to be alive and not know why you were given life. A meaningless life is one of the crises of modern society. Multiple studies have shown that a lack of purpose is linked to alcohol and drug abuse, depression, anxiety, and suicide.

> **The greatest tragedy in life is not death, but life without purpose.**

"I do not run like someone running aimlessly; I do not fight like a boxer beating the air."[7]

Now we have established that all life has been designed for meaning and purpose, let's continue to discover what that is.

Chapter 2

Discovering Your Life Purpose

"In the cemetery is buried the greatest treasure of untapped potential."
– Myles Munroe

Where are you on your journey to discovering and fulfilling your life purpose?

- Dead end – no idea what I'm called to do with my life

- Lost – I have an idea of my purpose but I need clarity and confidence

19

- Going in circles – caught in confusion, no longer sure what I should be doing, feel like I'm all over the place

- Stalled out – I know my purpose but need a jump start to get me going again in the right direction

- Full steam ahead – know exactly what I'm called to do and I'm doing it.

If you already know your life purpose and are living it, you probably won't be reading this book. I will therefore assume you relate to one of the other stages highlighted above.

Finding out your life purpose is a journey and a process that can begin anytime. If you have yet to embark on this journey of discovery, it can begin right now.

As a trained life coach I've read a number of self-help books on personal development and discovering your life purpose. The steps are essentially the same:

- Consider your dreams
- Determine your strengths and what you are good at
- Aim high
- Align with your values
- Set some goals and develop a plan of action
- Connect with others
- Go for it!
- Stay with the course, don't give up and finish well
- Leave a legacy and celebrate your successes.

These are all good principles, mostly based on the Bible, and will often lead to successful outcomes. We can learn much from them and I incorporate many of the principles into my coaching and leadership training.

However, because by definition self-help books are written from a self-centred viewpoint, they overlook a critical starting-point.

What matters most is not what *I want* to do or be, but discovering *the purpose I was designed for*.

A Higher Purpose

The question we have to ask ourselves is whether there is a higher purpose beyond myself, even a divine purpose?

If my complexity reveals a Designer and higher power, *why* was I created and designed to be the unique person that I am?

> **What matters most is not what *I want* to do or be, but discovering *the purpose I was designed for*.**

"Focusing on ourselves will never reveal our life's purpose."[8]

Some parents tell their children, 'You can be anything you want to be.' The question becomes, 'What do *you love* to do?' In other words, follow your passions. However, in the real world passion by itself is not enough. How many boys dream of becoming a professional footballer, only to discover as they get older that they just can't match what they see their favourite players doing on TV.

Others say, 'You can be anything your strengths allow you to be.' The question becomes, 'What *comes easily* to you?' In other words, follow your talents. While using a talent is commendable, what if you don't have the passion and motivation to use the talent and ability that you possess?

For people of faith, there is another dimension to the equation. The biblical perspective is, 'You can be all that God has created you to be!' In other words, follow your calling or vocation.

As we will see, following your passions and talents are important keys to unlocking your life purpose. But, the very best is to discover how these fit within a greater and higher purpose.

Ask, Hear & Respond

God calls people on an individual basis. The Bible shows this to be the case. He didn't speak to everyone from a burning bush. Only to Moses.

However He chooses to interact with us, our part is to ask, hear, and respond to what He says. A sense of calling is like having inner guidance, being directed by our own internal GPS.

The word, 'vocation' refers to the 'big picture' and is derived from the Latin word '*vocare*' which means 'to call'. Our vocation must incorporate our 'calling', 'purpose', 'mission', and 'destiny'.

It is what you are doing in life that makes a difference, that builds meaning for you, and that leaves a legacy. Our vocation and calling is when we discover our part in God's overall purpose.[9]

Can I Choose My Purpose?

'You may choose your career, your spouse, your hobbies, and many other parts of your life, but you don't get to choose your purpose.'[10]

We didn't get to choose our parents, our nationality, our gender, or much of our upbringing. In the same way, we don't choose our unique design and purpose. Our Creator did that long before we were born.

However, *it is up to us to first discover and then align our life with that purpose or not.* We get to choose whether to follow our Designer's purpose for our lives, or do our own thing.

This brings us back to the question about the meaning of life? Is there one and if so, is it about you or some higher purpose? Your answer will depend on your worldview.

How Worldview Impacts Life Purpose

I believe the only worldview that supports a clear life-purpose, not only for us as individuals, but also for the whole universe, is a biblical one that acknowledges a divine Creator, a created order, and an *eternal* purpose and destiny.

The Buddha stated, *'I don't exist. Therefore the ultimate purpose of my life is to cease to exist, to find Nirvana or eternal death to the illusion of existence.'*

Under Buddhism, we can make one life truly meaningful by using it to achieve 'Buddhahood' and so, when we die, escape the wheel of Samsāra. We escape the meaninglessness of it all.[11]

The Samsāra doctrine of cyclic existence is a central tenet of Indian religions, namely Jainism, Buddhism, Sikhism and Hinduism. There is no purpose to the whole wheel of Samsāra (process of reincarnation and aimless drifting) - being born, suffering, dying, being reborn, suffering, dying, being reborn, and so on.

The French existentialist philosopher, Jean-Paul Sartre, stated, *'No one created you for any purpose. Therefore, you are free to choose any purpose for your purposeless, meaningless life.'* According to his theory, life has no intrinsic meaning or value. You may choose a purpose for your life but ultimately, it has no point to it.

However, the Christian Bible affirms human purpose in two ways.

Firstly, mankind was made in God's image and was created so we could enjoy relationship with Him. Although the perfect creation was corrupted by man's rebellion, Jesus came and through His sacrificial death and resurrection, proclaimed that the kingdom of God had come to Earth so that all that had been broken would be restored.

Secondly, as individuals, God has a unique purpose for our lives. The Bible states, *'For we are God's handiwork, created in Christ Jesus to do good works, which God prepared in advance for us to do.'*[12]

We are therefore exhorted to steward and use the gifts and talents that we have been entrusted with, for God's glory and to extend His kingdom on Earth.

You were made for such a time as this!

Not only will we be the most effective and fulfilled when we live according to our God-given design, our life story is to be a part of the grand story that God is writing.

Our mission is to be a part of God's mission purpose.

Once we understand this, the vital question becomes, 'What is *my place* in God's story?'

> **We are made to live for something *bigger than ourselves* which is the kingdom of God.**

We are made to live for something *bigger than ourselves* which is the kingdom of God. We are to bring and advance God's kingdom on Earth.

Our lives here on Earth can have *eternal significance* as we live in the light of eternity and invest today in God's kingdom that will never end and last forever.[13]

Know the Designer

Before focusing on what we should *do*, we need to take a step back and consider a more fundamental issue.

Before discovering my design and purpose, it is incumbent upon us to first know *who* designed and created us in the first place.

The Shorter Westminster Catechism states man's chief-end to be to 'glorify God and enjoy Him forever'.

Once we know the one who designed and created us, we can then glorify Him by using what He has given us. We can truly be the person He has created us to be.

Use What You Have been Given

So the question we then need to ask ourselves is:

What's in your hand to use?

What have you been given?

How have you been hard-wired?

How have you been shaped?

In my book, *Empowered! Discovering Your Place in God's Story,* I use the acronym, S.H.A.P.E., which Rick Warren uses in his best-selling book, *The Purpose-Driven Life: What On Earth Am I Here For?*

However, I uniquely adapted his usage to make spiritual gifts (the 'S' in the acronym) applicable to *anyone* and for use in *any area* of life, not just within a church context which wouldn't apply to the majority of people.[14]

The P.U.R.P.O.S.E. Profile©

I have since developed my own acronym, P.U.R.P.O.S.E.©, which is more comprehensive than S.H.A.P.E., as follows:

Passions

Uniqueness

Relationships

Personality

Origins

Skills/Abilities

Experiences

Let's look at them one-by-one in more detail.

These constitute the 7 keys to unlocking your life purpose!

P.U.R.P.O.S.E.
Profile

7 Keys to Unlocking Your Life P.U.R.P.O.S.E.

Chapter 3

Key #1 - PASSIONS

The first key to unlock your life purpose is to turn to your heart and consider your passions.

In the Bible the word 'heart' is used to refer to a person's desires, passions, motivations, interests, and dreams. It is what gives us energy and meaning, what we care about, enjoy and love to do.

In whatever context, if someone has a desire which causes some strong feeling or emotion, we define this in terms of passion.

To identify our life passions, we need to move away from our mind and self-limiting beliefs, to what is in our heart.

Your feelings, not your mind, are more akin to your inner GPS.

Connect with Your Feelings

Ask yourself *how you feel* when you do something, e.g. play the guitar, paint a picture, give a talk? By

What makes you *feel really alive?*

connecting with your feelings (heart), you reveal your passions.

What makes you *feel really alive*?

Give yourself time to think and meditate about what is deep within. It may take time for it to surface.

Key Questions

Here are some other questions to help you identify your heart passions:

- What did you dream about becoming when you were a child? What did you enjoy doing before life (and systems) got in the way?

- What do you love to talk about the most? What could you talk about for hours on end?

- What subject could you research for hours or read numerous books on without getting bored?

- What do you *love* to do when you have free time? What areas of life are you naturally drawn to? What would you like to share with the world?

- When you connect with your heart and your feelings, what energises you and makes you come alive?

- You are totally 'in your element' and time seems to have disappeared. What are you doing?

- How would your life change if you suddenly inherited several million pounds? If money was not an issue, what would you do?

- If someone were to pay all of your living costs and expenses for two years, what work would you pursue in that time? [If you can't imagine not doing something, it's a passion. It doesn't have to be a moneymaker. Make your money some way that will give you the time for what you really love to do.]

- You can invite 5 people (whether alive or deceased) to a dinner party. Who would you choose? What is it about them that sparks something within you?

- What would you do if you knew you could not fail? If you were to pioneer a cause that was guaranteed to succeed, what would it be?

- It's your birthday and somebody offers to buy you an annual magazine subscription of your choice. What would you choose?

- Is there an issue that really grieves your heart? [what grieves you is a clue to something you may be assigned to address].

- Is there an issue that you hate and get really angry about?

- If you could write your own obituary summary, what would you like it to say?

- What difference do you want to make in the world? What legacy would you like to leave behind? [see Obituary Exercise in Appendix 1]

- If you were to die tomorrow, what would you regret not doing with your life?

- What would you do and how would you spend your time if you learned today that you only had five years left to live?

The passions in your heart are a key to unlocking your life purpose.

Chapter 4

Key # 2 -
UNIQUENESS

"Your time is limited, so don't waste it living someone else's life." – Steve Jobs

The second key to unlocking your life purpose is to consider your uniqueness.

Here are some popular affirmations that support our unique selves. Although many of us like the sentiment, we often struggle with actually living them out.

Be Yourself! (Why do we want to be like others?)

Dare to be different! (Why do we want to be the same?)

Stand out from the crowd! (Why do we work so hard to fit in?)

Swim against the tide! (Why do we tend to go with the flow?)

One of my daughter's favourite books growing up had the title: "You're Born an Original (Don't Die a Copy)."[15]

God didn't clone, He created. He made everything unique.

Every snowflake.

Every zebra stripe.

Every fingerprint.

Actually, there are other body parts that are also completely unique, even with identical twins:

...your iris (the best way to distinguish between identical twins),

...ear (both the geometric features as well as the faint sounds within ear cavities),

...lip print,

...tongue,

...voice (an essential requirement for voice recognition technology to be viable),

...toe print,

...teeth,

...retina,

...your gait (how you walk, use your feet),

...nose pores,

...and natural body odour!

As time goes by, science discovers we are even more unique than originally thought.[16]

To other people and to ourselves, we can appear like everyone else.

We can be replaced at work. We can be replaced by the one we love.

However, the truth is that we are *not the same* as other people.

We are *completely unique*.

We were made that way by our Creator. We are His masterpiece. His work of art.[17]

We are carefully planned, designed, and special.

Think about this question. Intrinsically, do you feel as though you were actually *born* to do a particular thing?

We are unique:

...in the way we perceive and experience things,

...in how we think and feel,

...in how we view life,

...in what we believe,

...in our genetics,

...and in how we're creative.

Some are good with improvising, some at inventing, some at creating, some at envisioning.

What fundamental beliefs do you feel truly passionate about?

Which jobs would encompass them?

> **The world doesn't need more of the same. It needs variety and difference. It needs you.**

Being unique is seen as something positive and to be celebrated, but why is it seldom practiced?

Instead, conformity is often seen as the goal as we fear being rejected or not being appreciated.

When we do have the courage to be who we truly are, our authenticity will be appreciated and we will make a greater impression, and be remembered for standing out above the crowd.

The world doesn't need more of the same. It needs variety and difference.

It needs you.

What makes you *uniquely you* is a combination of a number of things.

This includes your calling or vocation, your core beliefs and faith, and the values that you hold dear.

Core Values

Your core values are an expression of who you are right now. They point to who you truly are. They are an expression of what you believe and help to determine your priorities in life.

Most of us don't know our values or what is most important to us. Often, we focus on what our society, culture, and media values.

Creating a list of personal, core values can be a daunting prospect. You can find lists of values online although selecting from predetermined lists is not the best approach. Our values need to be *discovered* and revealed.

However, to help give you a sense of what your values may encompass, here *are* some prompts:

> acceptance,
> beauty,
> creativity,
> empowerment,
> equality,
> family,
> freedom,
> health,
> honour,
> integrity,
> stewardship.

Consider the following:

What do you believe?

What is the fruit of the values you believe in?

What are your 5 most important values in life?

-

-

-

-

-

What would you pay for, sacrifice for, suffer for and even die for?

What would you stand up for or refuse to lie down for?

Another way of asking this question is:

What men and women, living or dead, do you most admire and why?

What values, qualities or virtues do they have that you respect and you look up to?

Addressing the above questions is the starting point for determining your values.

Values drive and motivate people's behaviour and what we do will either align with our life purpose or not.

When a person's actions don't match their values (e.g. valuing family but working too much; valuing integrity but agreeing to bend the rules), they are likely to become discontented.

Only when we live and work in complete *alignment* with our core values – our inner life and outer life being in alignment - will we experience peace and satisfaction.

Our life purpose will never be out of alignment with our values and character, or our beliefs and faith.

The degree to which we live our lives consistent with high, life-enhancing values, is the measure of our character.

Don't let your talents and gifting take you where your character cannot keep you.

Character is a key to us living a life of purpose.

Our values should always support and contribute to fulfilling our life purpose.

The process of clarifying our core values is not always easy. Selecting values from a list seldom works as people often choose values that are deemed socially acceptable, rather than discover the values that are already at the core of their being.

Value Clarification Exercise

Here is an exercise that can help you clarify and articulate your core values.

Using either a computer or a pencil (with rubber/eraser), begin to write several words together (most significant at the beginning) to form a string describing the value. For example:

- Integrity/honesty/authenticity
- Leadership/empower/release

It is unlikely you will be able to list all your core values in one sitting. It will take time to identify a complete list of your core values.

To help with this exercise, think about key moments in your life where a particular value came to the forefront. Ask yourself what value was being honoured at that specific moment in time.

Remember that these key moments may be a positive or negative experience. It maybe that a core value resonated with you following an experience or event that caused you pain, frustration, or anger.

Once you have brainstormed a number of values, rank the top ten in priority order.

1.

2.

3.

4.

5.

6.

7.

8.

9.

10.

Core Beliefs

Core beliefs are the essence of how we see *ourselves*, *others*, *the world*, and *the future*.

Beneath what we think on the surface, our core beliefs are what we hold to be absolute truths deep within us.

Depending on what we have been taught and our self-perceptions, sometimes our beliefs can promote well-being; sometimes they can be destructive and perpetuate self-abuse ('self-limiting beliefs').

Negative perceptions can become 'self-fulfilling prophecies' where we look for evidence that supports our idea, which then reinforces the belief and results in it coming to pass (e.g. if you think you are not a likeable person it will be more difficult to make friends).

They determine how we perceive and interpret the world and will influence our understanding of our unique life purpose.

What we believe typically begins in childhood and is influenced strongly by our family of origin (see chapter 7).

They can also be affected by teachers and peers, and by our experiences in life (see chapter 9).

What Are Your Core Beliefs?

To identify your core beliefs you may need to keep a journal and record your thoughts over a period of time.

What you really believe may seem to fluctuate when you experience a flux of emotion, so take note for those deeper, more serious beliefs that often emerge when you are not being emotional.

I am ...
e.g. 'I am blessed', 'I am inadequate', 'I don't deserve happiness', 'I am unlovable', 'I can make a difference'

Others are ...
e.g. 'people are essentially good', 'people always reject me', 'people can't be trusted'

The world is ...
e.g. 'the world is a dangerous place', 'the world is a safe place', 'the world is going to get better'

The future is ...
e.g. 'the future is hopeless', 'the future is bright'

Reflect on how you see yourself, other people, the world, and the future.

What do you see?

Write or type out your core beliefs.

<u>Yourself</u>

<u>Others</u>

<u>The World</u>

<u>The Future</u>

Sometimes our core beliefs will be challenged. Sometimes they may need to become more balanced.

For example, instead of, 'No one likes my ideas' to 'Not everyone will like my ideas all the time, but my ideas will be appreciated by some people.'

Instead of, 'The world is just going to get worse and worse' to 'We cannot create a utopia, but we can work towards many positive transformations in the world'.

Discovering and clarifying our beliefs and values, those things which are at the core of our being, will highlight some key aspects of what makes us unique as a person.

In doing so, we will move closer to discovering and fulfilling our life purpose.

Chapter 5

Key #3 - RELATIONSHIPS

In this chapter we will consider the third key to unlocking our life purpose – our relationships.

Just as we need to pay attention to both our inner life and outer life, and ensure they are in alignment, our life purpose can be viewed in two ways.

Inner Purpose

We have both an *inner* purpose (our being) and an *outer* purpose (our doing). If the doing becomes much greater than our being, it typically results in burnout and exhaustion.

We must therefore pay attention to and not neglect our inner, internal purpose.

Ultimately, our purpose is inward, related to who we are and who we are intended to be.

When the inner and outer purposes are in alignment, then we will be balanced and whole people.

In giving focus to our inner purpose, our *primary relationship* is with our Creator, the one who designed us.

If we get to know Him, it will be easier to discover our purpose in life as He knows us better than we even know ourselves.

Jesus never gave His disciples a big task or commission before inviting them into a relationship with Him.

He first gave them an *identity*, then envisioned them with a *vision* for their life, and then *commissioned* them to invest their lives in bringing it to pass.

Any good work that we're engaged in must never become more important than our relationship with our Creator. Otherwise we can quickly risk burnout or simply lose the joy of knowing Him. As the Shorter Westminster Catechism so aptly put it, 'Man's chief end is to glorify God and *enjoy Him* forever!'

With that as a foundation, we can then reach out and develop other relationships with other people.

We are relational beings. Our relationships with other people are key to us both discovering and fulfilling our purpose.

No man is an island and we were never designed to live or manage life by ourselves.

In China, a person's connections or relationships is referred to as 'guanxi'. You cannot do without it, especially in business.

> **The resources we need to fulfil our life purpose will come through people.**

For any of us, our relationships are vitally important as no matter how self-sufficient we try to become, we need others.

Our Resources are in Our Relationships

Relationships are vital not only for love, friendship, companionship, and having fun, but also because *the resources we need to fulfil our life purpose will come through people.*

To help us discover our life purpose we should therefore consider the relationships we have in our lives, both past and present.

Where would we be without them?

> **What influences, whether positive or negative, have others had on making you the person you are today?**

Think about how other people have helped you get to the point you are at now.

What influences, whether positive or negative, have others had on making you the person you are today?

When we think of slavery being outlawed in the British Empire, the name that usually comes to mind is

William Wilberforce. However, he may never have spearheaded this work without the influence of some significant people in his life. One was John Newton, the former slave-trader who penned the hymn, 'Amazing Grace'. The other was William Penn, a classmate who later became Britain's Prime Minister. Newton encouraged Wilberforce to view his political work as a divine calling on his life. Penn challenged him to present to the British Parliament a motion on the subject of the slave trade.

Other people shape us. Sometimes they inspire or challenge us. Sometimes they treat us badly but even then, such experiences can cause us to get stronger.

Every relationship, whether with parents, spouse, children, siblings, friends, or work colleague, carries with it the potential for growth.

Different people play different roles within our lives.

Not every relationship is meant to last a lifetime. Once the purpose is fulfilled, often such relationships end.

An ended relationship is not necessarily a failure. It might just be a natural course of events. As some relationships come to an end, new ones emerge.

Our relationships, both past and present, are a key to unlocking our life purpose.

They are also important in us bringing that purpose and assignment to pass.

7 Keys to Unlocking Your Life P.U.R.P.O.S.E.

Chapter 6

Key # 4 - PERSONALITY

The fourth key to unlocking our life purpose is personality.

In everyday life we often like to describe or assess other people's personalities.

We may refer to someone as having 'a great personality', or that they got their personality from their dad or mum. Such observations are usually based on how we view people's characteristics and behaviour.

While there is no single agreed upon definition of personality, it is often

71

thought that personality is a consistent set of characteristics and tendencies that influence how we think, feel and behave as people.

Current research indicates that our personality is a result of both genetic and environmental factors.

> *Different personalities are suited to different roles and purposes in life.*

Different personalities are suited to different roles and purposes in life.

There are no "right" or "wrong" temperaments. However, our specific personality traits do impact different areas of our lives, such as how we relate to others, how we gather and process information, and how we make decisions. Our personality can also affect our health and well-being.

There are many different theories about personality and numerous attempts have been made to measure it.

While not an exact science, personality assessments have their merits and can aid us in self-discovery.

Some popular assessments include:

1. *The Myers-Briggs Type Indicator (MBTI)*

This assessment is based on the work of psychoanalyst, Carl Jung.

Jung thought that people understood the world through sensation and intuition (which helps *perception*) and, feeling and thinking (which support *judgment*). Jung suggested that only one of these psychological functions is powerful most of the time.

This personality type assessment also shows if people are extraverts or introverts.

The MBTI measures preferences with 16 personality types across the four scales:

Extravert/Introvert - are you outwardly or inwardly focused?

If you could be described as talkative and outgoing, you like to be in a fast-paced environment, tend to think out loud and work out ideas with other people, and enjoy being the centre of attention...then you prefer *Extraversion*.

If, on the other hand, you are more reserved and private, prefer a slower pace with time for contemplation, tend to think things through inside your head, and would rather observe than be the centre of attention...then you prefer *Introversion*.

You may, of course, be a mix of the two. Most people will generally have an overall preference for one or the other.

Sensing/iNtuition - how do you prefer to absorb information?

If when gathering information you tend to focus on the reality of how things are, pay attention to concrete facts and details, prefer ideas that have practical applications, and like to describe things in a specific, literal way, then you prefer *Sensing*.

If, however, you like to imagine the possibilities of how things could be, notice the big picture and how everything connects, enjoy ideas and concepts, and like to describe things in more figurative ways, then you prefer *iNtuition* (abbreviated by the letter N).

Thinking/Feeling - how do you prefer to make decisions?
If you make decisions in an impersonal way, using logical reasoning, value justice and fairness, enjoy finding the flaws in an argument, and could be described as reasonable and level-headed, you prefer *Thinking*.

If you base your decisions on personal values and how your actions affect others, value harmony and forgiveness, like to please others and point out the best in people, and could be described as warm and empathetic, you prefer *Feeling*.

Perception/Judging – how do you prefer to live in your outer life?

If you're a person who likes to have matters settled, thinks rules and deadlines should be respected, prefers to have detailed, step-by-step instructions, makes plans and want to know what you're getting into, you prefer *Judging*.

If you prefer to leave your options open, see rules and deadlines as flexible, like to improvise and make things up as you go, and are spontaneous, enjoy surprises and new situations, then you prefer *Perceiving*.

Based on an individual's responses to the MBTI questionnaire, the point score will result in one of the following four letter combinations. A person who prefers Introversion, Sensing, Thinking, and Judging is referred to as an ISTJ. There are 16 possible combinations or types.

- **INTJ:** Imaginative and strategic thinkers, who are good at planning

- **INTP:** Innovative inventors with a thirst for knowledge

- **ENTJ:** Confident and imaginative leaders

- **ENTP:** Smart and curious individuals, who love an intellectual debate or challenge

- **INFJ:** Quiet but inspiring

- **INFP:** Considerate and always willing to help a good cause

- **ENFJ**: Inspiring leaders who are good at captivating their audience

- **ENFP:** Enthusiastic, creative and sociable individuals who boost the mood of those around them

- **ISTJ:** Practical and can always be relied on

- **ISFJ**: Dedicated and willing to defend those they care about

- **ESTJ:** Good at managing projects or people

- **ESFJ:** Caring, sociable and popular individuals, who are eager to help others out

- **ISTP:** Experimenters, who can master all tools

- **ISFP:** Creative types, who are always up for trying something new

- **ESTP:** Energetic and perceptive individuals who like to take risks

- **ESFP:** Full on enthusiasm, keeping life fun and interesting.

2. *DISC Assessment*

DISC evaluates behaviour and focuses on the personality traits of Dominance, Influence, Steadiness, and Conscientiousness (DISC).

The DISC questionnaire seeks to find out how you respond to challenges, how you influence others, how you respond to rules and procedures, and about your preferred pace of activity. It does not measure every dimension of your personality.

A number of questionnaires identify personality based on the four basic temperaments described by the Greek philosopher, Hippocrates: choleric, sanguine, phlegmatic, and melancholy.

D – Dominance (choleric)

– people who are typically forceful, direct, like to take charge, enjoys challenges and problem solving; seek control

I – Influence (sanguine)

– people who are typically optimistic, motivational, friendly and talkative; seek recognition

S – Steadiness (phlegmatic)

– people who are typically steady, patient, loyal, cooperative and practical, good team player; seek acceptance

C – Conscientious (melancholic)

– people who are typically precise, diplomatic, sensitive and analytical; seek accuracy.

3. *The Enneagram*

This is a model of 9 personality types where one is a dominant personality type, complemented by another "wing" element which makes up a second side to your personality.

Type 1 – *The Reformer, Perfectionist* – making things right in the world. Ones are motivated by the need to live life the right way, to improve themselves and others.

Type 2 – *The Helper, Giver* – the needs and wants of others. Twos are motivated by the need to be loved and appreciated and are typically warm, generous, and caring.

Type 3 – *The Achiever, Motivator* – succeeding by getting things done. Threes are motivated by the need to be productive, to achieve success, and avoid failure.

Type 4 – *The Individualist, Romantic* – being special and unique. Fours are motivated by the need to understand deeply their feelings and avoid appearing ordinary.

Type 5 – *The Investigator, Observer* – learning all there is to know. Fives are motivated by the need to know everything which gives them a sense of security.

Type 6 – *The Loyalist, Questioner* – being the devil's advocate. Sixes are motivated by the need for security, order, and certainty.

Type 7 – *The Enthusiast, Adventurer* – enjoying and experiencing life. Sevens are motivated by the need to be happy and enjoy life.

Type 8 – *The Challenger, Protector* – being strong and in control. Eights are motivated by the need to be against something, standing up for truth and justice.

Type 9 – *The Peacemaker, Mediator* – maintaining peace and harmony. Nines are motivated by the need to keep the peace and to avoid conflict.

If you search online, you will be able to take the personality assessments highlighted above.

When we understand our personality we not only improve our self-awareness, we will also improve our effectiveness in fulfilling our life purpose.

We will know what works best with our personality and what doesn't work as well.

As your life purpose will take account of your personality, it is important that we understand this key part of who we are.

7 Keys to Unlocking Your Life P.U.R.P.O.S.E.

Chapter 7

Key # 5 - ORIGINS

Title fifth key to unlocking your life purpose is to look at your origins.

You are not a product of chance or the result of some cosmic accident.

Whether your parents wanted you or not, you are your Creator's workmanship and were born for a reason and specific purpose, even though it may not be immediately apparent to you right now.

Even the circumstances of your birth, your parents and ethnic origin, where you were born and the generation in which you came into the Earth, none of these things were accidental. There is a purpose behind them.

Although we had no choice in these things, they constitute our sovereign foundations, on which our life is built.

I do not believe that it was the Creator's original plan for anyone to suffer. But we know many do and some never have the opportunity to experience the purpose in life that was destined for them. The world is no longer a perfect place. At the same time, sometimes beauty can come out of the ashes. Hardship, pain, and suffering can result in some people doing amazing things with their lives.

When we consider family upbringing, children who experience more positive interactions in their early years go on to be healthier and more successful in school and in life. Unfortunately, the opposite is true as well.

Poverty, exposure to family violence, and lack of access to quality early learning experiences can negatively impact a child's early brain development, and subsequently, their long-term success.[18]

However, often such negative experiences can become a springboard to a person's destiny later in life.

In some cases it can make the person stronger, more compassionate, resilient and more used to having to deal with life's challenges.

Jesus began his life on Earth in a stinky manger. He then spent time as a refugee in a foreign land.

Life doesn't need a perfect beginning to live out your life purpose.

Family of Origin

The way we see ourselves, others, and the world, is shaped in the setting of our family of origin (i.e. the family in which you grew up).

The views we develop there, stay with us throughout our life.[19] Our family of origin has an enormous influence over our beliefs, expectations, and behaviour as adults.

> **The way we see ourselves, others, and the world, is shaped in the setting of our family of origin.**

Worldview

Our view of the world, what we believe and have faith in, what we hold deep convictions about, are often a result of our family upbringing, as this is where our early formation takes place.

While post-modernity has sought to discredit truth, a belief in actual objective truth will provide a bedrock and measure by which we can fulfil the very purpose of our existence.

Everyone lives out their worldview beliefs in life.

A worldview answers fundamental questions such as:

- Why are we here?

- What is the meaning and purpose of life?

- Is there a difference between right and wrong?

- Is there a God?

Our worldview not only reflects what we think the world is like (what we perceive to be real), it directs what we think the world should be like (prescribes how we act and respond to life).[20]

There are essentially three major worldviews:

- *Secularism* (or secular humanism): the atheistic belief

that there is no God or spiritual dimension (ultimate reality is physical)

- *Animism* (which would include Hinduism, Buddhism, and eastern folk): the belief that the world is ultimately spiritual, in which the physical world is animated by spirits or gods (ultimate reality is spiritual)

- *Theism*: the belief in one personal, infinite God (ultimate reality is personal).

Every person and society can be found somewhere along a continuum, with secularism and animism at either end and with theism in the middle.

Our worldview is not only critical to how we see reality and understand life, it also shapes our place in the world and our view of the future. This, in turn, will have a huge impact on how we come to an understanding of our life purpose.

92

Understanding Family Messages

It can be difficult to know the extent of its influence as so much of what we learn in the family is unconscious. Much of our learning becomes a part of our emotional and social DNA.

In order to understand how our family of origin impacts on our life purpose, you may like to consider the following:

Family Genogram

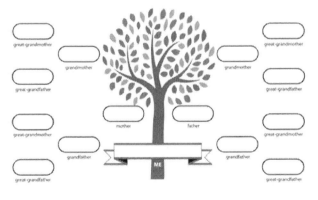

www.FreeFamilyTreeTemplates.com

- Produce a family genogram to discover and analyse what people in your family history did with their lives.

- Are there any recurring themes?

- Are there skills or talents that can be seen in several generations of your family?

- Ask your parents (if possible) about their work and why they came to do that?

What was their plan?

Did they have any sense of calling or vocation?

- Look back into your ancestry as far as you can for people who have had a significant gift or talent, yet never lived up to their potential.

  Maybe there is a connection in an area that you can pick up the baton and continue?

- Be open to family or generational callings and life assignments. Explore each other's dreams and look for overlap.

Chapter 8

Key # 6 –
SKILLS & ABILITIES

The sixth key to unlocking our life purpose is to consider your skills and abilities. If you're a person of faith you may also want to look at your 'spiritual gifts'.

These things taken together are your 'gift mix' and give you the power and means to fulfil your life purpose.

Skills

Unlike your innate abilities, skills are acquired and learnt over time. Skills are

97

those function-driven tasks or specific activities that you have learnt to do well.

Some skills can be transferred and used in a variety of jobs and situations. They can also vary widely in terms of complexity (e.g. 'typing' and 'performing brain surgery').

> **Your skills and abilities give you the power and means to fulfil your life purpose.**

Skills can be viewed in a number of categories. The simplest way is perhaps the following two categories:

- *Hard skills* – tangible and measurable such as: typing, reading, writing, carpentry, proficiency in a foreign language, computing, and accounting.

- *Soft skills* – intangible and harder to measure such as:
  - creativity, critical thinking, and problem-solving;

- interpersonal skills including leadership, teamwork, diplomacy, and negotiation;
- communication skills including persuasion, listening, and humour;
- emotional skills such as managing stress, adapatability, and resilience.

Your 'Hard' Skills:

Your 'Soft' Skills:

A skills inventory is a useful addition to your toolbox in determining what you can do. Skill gaps can be addressed by getting the required training or experience. An inability to acquire a certain skill can also provide useful information in unlocking your life purpose.

Natural Abilities

Our natural abilities and talents are what we were born with and what developed during our formative years growing up as children.

Unlike skills which are learned and acquired throughout our lives, abilities are our God-given "hard-wiring" and are clear indicators of what we are called to do.

Have you ever been in some kind of team where you had to take a role that did not suit you?

For example, a wrong position in a sports team, being asked to play the guitar when you are really a drummer, being asked to do the accounts when you love to teach? This can be made worse when you see somebody else doing badly the thing you know you are really good at and should have been asked to do!

In recent years it has become popular to identify one's strengths.

Research indicates that fewer than a quarter of us actually play to our strengths.

The natural abilities you have been equipped with are not without reason. They have not been given to you in order to go to waste. There is a purpose behind them.

What You Do Best

Find out what you do well and do more of it; find out what you don't do well and stop doing it.

As we do so, we will align ourselves with whom we have been made to be. We will also become more effective in what we do.

How can you discover what you do best?

One way would be to ask some people who know you really well what they consider your talents to be.

You can also consider yourself what naturally flows for you without you even having to try?

The very best way of determining your innate abilities is to take the Highlands Ability Battery™.

As a certified Highlands Consultant, I have been trained to take you through this powerful assessment and provide the follow-up session that will help you make sense of your own ability profile. Just get in touch and I can arrange this for you (see back of book for contact details).

The Highlands Ability Battery is unique among assessment tools because it provides *objective* measurements of natural abilities. Because it does not depend on self-reporting or on subjective appraisals, it gives you a clear and powerful picture of who you really are.[21]

Once identified, as good stewards of what we have been given we should also seek to develop our talents with appropriate skills. These will enhance our natural abilities.

Spiritual Gifts

If you have a biblical worldview you may wish to take my unique Spiritual Gifts Questionnaire.[22]

Most Bible scholars classify spiritual gifts into three categories: ministry gifts, motivational gifts, and manifestation gifts.[23] These 'charismata' gifts have been given to serve one another and to advance God's kingdom.

In this book we will consider the first two categories of gifts.

Ministry gifts are given to facilitate and assist people to work out their particular callings and life purpose. Typically, they are only viewed within a church context.

However, given that most people's purpose will primarily function outside of the religious sphere of life, it can be helpful to expand the terminology beyond that used in scripture, as highlighted below.

Apostolic (Entrepreneur, Visionary, Pioneer, Innovator, Strategist, Activist):

People with this gift take the lead in pioneering or overhauling initiatives that have lost a sense of purpose and direction. Whereas, in a church context, people with this gift may be planting churches, in another context, they may be starting new businesses or pioneering innovative initiatives to solve problems.

Prophetic (Perceiver, Inspirer, Consultant, Advocate, Troubleshooter, Questioner, Non-conformist, Reformer, Radical, Revolutionary):

These people act like a mouthpiece, pointing to the future and bringing words of correction and challenge. They can often get into trouble as they see things that others don't and speak with boldness and insight. They typically demonstrate moral courage and an uncompromising commitment to worthy values.

Evangelistic (Communicator, Networker, Recruiter, Reconciler):

This gift is really a 'selling' ability and can use different forms of communication including speaking, music, drama, and other creative ways.

Shepherd/Pastoral (Care-giver, Guide, Mentor, Nurturer, Humanizer):

People with this gift are called to stay in a place in order to nurture, guide and care for others, and help them grow.

Teaching (Instructor, Educator, Trainer, Researcher):

This gifting enables people to impart understanding and clarity, providing clear instruction that results in understanding information or truth. They can also impart tools so people can grow and be the people they need to be.

Helping (Helpers, Servers, Doers):

People with this gift have a strong desire to serve others. They may fulfil significant responsibilities as a loyal #2 person, and take effective action to provide for the practical, physical needs of others.

Giving (Sharers, Contributors):

People with the gift of giving respond with wisdom to special needs by giving or investing in people or projects.

Exhortation (Exhorters, Encouragers):

Exhorters and Encouragers catalyse personal development out of a keen awareness of a person's growth needs.

Leadership/Administration/ Facilitation/Management:

Leaders, Facilitators, Administrators, Managers, and Owners cast vision, enlist others, and coordinate their efforts towards initiatives that fulfil a specific purpose; organise information, people, or resources to more efficiently accomplish goals or purposes.

Mercy (Compassion, Kindness):

People with the gift of Mercy, Compassion and Kindness suffer with, comfort, and provide hope for those who are in pain.

My Spiritual Gifts Questionnaire to help you identify your spiritual gifting can be found in Appendix 2 at the back of the book.

It is unique and different to other spiritual gift questionnaires which focus and limit gifting solely to a church meeting context. As a result, all Christian vocabulary has been removed and it is intended that the questions can apply to anyone, regardless of their sense of calling or life purpose.[24]

Please note that in practice, individuals will typically have a cluster or mix of gifts that will include dominant gifts supported by other strengths and gifting.

Chapter 9

Key # 7 –
EXPERIENCES

The seventh and final key to unlock your unique purpose in life is to consider your key life experiences.

In addition to our family of origin and other issues which define who we are from birth, there are other key life experiences that shape us.

Here are seven kinds of experiences that should be examined:

1. Family experiences
– values
– modeling

111

– heritage
– cultural background

2. *Educational experiences*
– favourite subjects and learning
– cross-cultural exposure
– life experiences
– what kind of knowledge did I acquire?

3. *Vocational experiences*
– effective and enjoyable jobs
– training received
– what have I done well?

4. Spiritual experiences
– meaningful encounters with God
– seeds of destiny?
– life calling scripture verses/prophetic words received?

5. Ministry experiences
– how served God in the past
– where has there been a sense of blessing and empowerment?

6. Painful experiences
 – problems, hurts, trials

7. Relational experiences
– friendships
– associations
– connections
– teachers/mentors
– role models?

> **The meaning we create from our experiences shape who we are.**

The meaning we create from our experiences shape who we are.

Two people may have a very similar experience but afford very different meanings to it. Because we get to create the meaning, we end up creating our own lives and who we become.

While we cannot always control what happens to us, we can always choose *how we react* to it.[25]

Looking at our experiences, both good and bad, recognises that we are more than just our talents, gifts, and interests. We are also who we are because of the successes and wounds we have experienced. Discovery has to be wholistic. Sometimes our life purpose can be discovered out of a time of suffering and difficulty.

Tell Your Story (group activity)

Each person has 10 minutes to draw their life story on a flip chart and 5 minutes to share with the group.

Reflection Questions

In addition, reflect on significant events and transitions (turning points) in your life.

How can your experiences help you impact the spheres of life and society where you live and work?

How can your credentials open up opportunities within your sphere(s) of influence or focus area?

How can you network with others of like mind to influence your sphere(s) of influence?

Reference Experiences

Reference experiences are key experiences or moments that change the way you view yourself as a person.

These experiences are powerful because they give you the confidence to know you can do something in a given situation. They help you create an identity of yourself, especially when they tap into your passion and talents.

Let me give an example from my own life. It's said that public speaking is one of the top fears for most people. Not being an extravert, I know it would have been a scary thing for me to do when I was growing up. However, once I managed to give a short talk at a youth meeting, I was then able to give another one. These experiences enabled me to keep giving talks, including to larger numbers of people. Each time, I had an experience to refer back to, to tell myself that I could do this, based on what I had managed to do before. After time, I was able to speak to hundreds of people. Today, if I feel the nerves before getting up to speak, I remind myself what I have done many times before. These experiences have shaped my identity and confirmed to myself that I am a teacher. I have preached in church meetings, I have given lectures to university students, I have run workshops. I can do this!

The key is to face your fears and to take action. You can read lots of books and learn the theory, but without having reference experiences under your belt, from having actually taken the action yourself, it won't mean much.

However, as we begin to take steps to walking in our purpose, these reference experiences will help us to continue to grow and gain the confidence to keep going.

P.U.R.P.O.S.E. Integration

7 Keys to Unlocking Your Life P.U.R.P.O.S.E.

Chapter 10

Personal Vision

Having used all 7 keys to unlock your life purpose, it is important to integrate all the discoveries that you have made.

One way to do this is to create a Personal Vision Statement or Vision Board.

A clear Personal Vision is an integration of your passions, uniqueness, relationships, personality, origins, skills & abilities, and experiences.

A Personal Vision or mission statement is a unique expression of what is important to you and serves as a guide to discovering and fulfilling your Life Purpose. It expresses how you commit to live your life.

It is a living document in that it should be reviewed on a regular basis and amended as necessary.

Articulating a Personal Vision can also help maintain balance in our lives.

Being Call & Doing Call

In Chapter 5 I stated that we have an inner purpose (our being) and an outer purpose (our doing). In articulating a Personal Vision or Calling it is helpful to distinguish between a Life Message (a being call) and a Life Task or Role (a doing call).[26]

If we focus solely on doing a particular task we can get caught up with getting all the details of the calling journey right (i.e. hearing correctly and making all the right choices). Instead, highlighting a calling as *a Message to be embodied and expressed* will free us from becoming overly focused on a specific task or location in order to live out our calling and life purpose. The task/role becomes a channel or means by which your Message is communicated to your audience.

Personal Vision Journal/Notebook

My specially designed Personal Vision Journal/Notebook is an ideal resource for those wishing to develop and record their own personal visions for their lives.

It would provide a valuable record as you work through the 7 keys outlined in this book (see the ad at the back of the book for further details).

Vision Board

Consider making a Vision Board which encapsulates your Life Purpose.

A Vision Board is an inspirational and motivational collage made up of pictures, images, affirmations, meaningful quotes or words spoken directly to you, which serve as an image of your future.

> **It is helpful to distinguish between a Life Message (a being call) and a Life Task (a doing call).**

It represents your Personal Vision and Life Purpose, your passions and goals, what you are aiming for, including how you feel about fulfilling it.

A Vision Board may be produced on card, paper, or on your computer. Templates and apps are available to help you get started.

Once completed, put your Vision Board in a place where you can see it on a daily, regular basis. It will serve as a powerful visualization tool to help keep you focused on seeing your Life Purpose come to pass.

Conclusion

Where Do I Go From Here?

Growing in self-awareness and discovering our God-given design and purpose for our lives is a process, sometimes a long one.

As you unlock and consider your Passions, Uniqueness, Relationships, Personality, Origins, Skills & Abilities, and Experiences, I believe your Life Purpose will begin to come into focus.

Write down and record the key insights you receive and pray over them. Share with a trusted friend. The support and affirmation of others can be very encouraging and sometimes they may recognize something in you that you do not see yourself.

Consider some coaching sessions to unpack things further. A coach should be able to help you bring all the pieces together so that you can begin to identify and articulate your life direction and purpose.

Transitioning into Your Life Purpose

Whatever purpose your life has been designed to serve, you need to understand that it will not happen automatically, just because you've been created and equipped for a particular task. You have to lay hold and grasp it, and make it your own.[27]

You also have to be intentional and take action so that you begin to live in alignment with your purpose.

> **You have to be intentional and take action in order to live in alignment with your purpose.**

Using the keys outlined in this book is really just the first step in unlocking the door to then begin walking towards or in your purpose.

For some of you, maybe there is a huge gap between where you are now, and where you want to be?

Develop a Strategy & Action Plan

"You need a plan to build a house. To build a life, it is even more important to have a plan." – Zig Ziglar

The next step is to set some goals and creating an action plan based on your purpose. This is really important as it will ensure you don't lose momentum and continue to move forward.

No matter where you are right now, begin to take steps, however small, towards living in alignment with your life purpose. Do what you can at this point in time.

Maybe you need to learn a new skill or receive some training? Maybe you should connect with other like-minded people who will encourage you as you move forward?

Consider having a coach to help you with your action plan and to give you some accountability.

It is almost inevitable that you will need to step out of your comfort zone.

Start taking steps, and trust the Lord as you go. This is what God essentially said to Abraham when He revealed to him his life purpose.[28] He had to step out of what was familiar and begin to venture into a new place without knowing the final destination.

If you are a Christian, begin using your gifts and all that you are to manifest the kingdom of God – His character, His justice, His wisdom, His healing, His truth, His creativity, etc.

Spheres of Influence

Appendix 3 includes a list of Focus Areas and Spheres of Influence. Consider and determine what particular sphere of society you have a passion for.

In what sphere or domain do you believe you are gifted?

In which spheres of society has God given you influence?

It may be helpful for you to review again the questions included in the chapter on 'Passions'. Describe that passion and consider how this passion can be used within your sphere(s) of influence for positive transformation.

Eternal Reward

Towards the beginning of this book I highlighted that, according to the Christian worldview, our individual life purpose is designed to contribute to a higher, divine purpose.

The Bible also makes clear that Jesus will one day return with rewards for those who have used the talents and gifts they've been given, and carried out the life purpose for which they have been designed. This is not about earning our salvation, but about how we have used what has been entrusted to us.

When the time comes to meet your Designer and Creator, will you be able to say, 'this is who you made me to be and I have sought to fulfill your purpose for my life'? If so, there will be great rejoicing!

In the meantime, being able to unlock your life purpose is where your life truly begins!

Appendices

Appendix 1
Obituary Exercise
(How Will You Be Remembered?)

The Man Who Read His Own Obituary

The Nobel Prize is one of the most recognisable and prestigious awards today, honouring men and women from around the world for outstanding achievements in different fields.

The founder of the awards, Alfred Nobel, was himself known for his many achievements and inventions, which included over 300 patents. However, the reason Nobel left most of his fortune to establishing the Nobel Foundation was because he wanted to change the way he would be remembered.

What caused this change was reading his own obituary after a French newspaper mistakenly published it after the death of Alfred's brother. The obituary was not pleasant reading as Alfred was described as 'The Merchant of Death', having invented dynamite and becoming rich by 'finding ways to kill more people faster than ever before.' To Alfred, reading his own obituary became a warning. It inspired him to change his life so he would be remembered for something good.

Be Warned!

This exercise also comes with a warning. This exercise is likely to significantly change your life!

But in order to obtain the benefit that will come from doing this, you first have to imagine that you are dead!

Yes, you read that correctly. This is a case of first having to die in order that you may live!

Many people have discovered that their life changed forever after doing this exercise. It comes in two parts and you will need to set aside some quality time in order to do it.

I want you to imagine that you are at the end of your life. I want you to look back and reflect on what you did with your life and time here on Earth.

Once you have done this I want you to write down two versions of your life.

YOUR NAME HERE

WHAT DO YOU WANT THIS TO SAY?

Lorem ipsum dolor sit amet, consectetur adipiscing elit. Duis molestie, lacus vitae vestibulum dictum, nibh libero suscipit augue, quis eleifend dolor augue vitae sed. Fusce et quam justo. Etiam dapibus lacinia metus, in mattis sapien tincidunt in. Phasellus eget varius nibh, eu aliquet augue. Sed sem nibh, volutpat nec elit fermentum, varius bibendum ipsum. Nulla et nunc scelerisque at mauris id. Euismo accumsan turpis. Suspendisse ac gravida libero, ac malesuada nisi. Proin imperdiet orci eu eu interdum mattis.

Curabitur dignissim lobortis justo nec sagittis. Cras pharetra elit ac eros elementum ultrices. Mauris quam augue, hendrerit et scelerisque scelerisque, vehicula ac eros. Sed ac lacinia diam. Mauris faucibus, nisi eget sceisgit scelerisque, lectus lacus pellentesque ante, sit amet varius tortor tellus et massa. Donec id pharetra dolor. In nec vulputate turpis, et ullamcorper sapien. Duis condimentum tortor nec turpis elementum tincidunt. Duis et orci nulla. Proin rutrum auctor id justo scelerisque, vitae facilisis nunc fermentum. Nulla tincidunt est id justo elementum, non lobortis neque vestibulum. Vivamus accumsan neque at sem molestie, ac lacus magna condimentum. Fusce nec ligula et lacus finibus vestibulum. Donec sapien augue, vehicula ut varius velit, suscipit quis orci.

In aliquet lectus ac augue molestie, et rutrum metus malesuada. Etiam luctus mi neque, nec luctus purus scelerisque in. Phasellus porttitor lacus sed nulla sagittis tincidunt. Proin at purus elementum, commodo nunc vitae, elementum quam. Vivamus ultricies lacus at sapien iaculis eleifend. Quisque ut amet varius purus interdum et malesuada fames ac ante ipsum primis in faucibus. Vestibulum posuere placerat malesuada.

29

Firstly, the life you wanted (your 'fantasy' obituary) or what you would want written about you when you have passed away many years from now.

Don't over-think this exercise. Do not edit, censor, analyze or critique your thoughts, but write what comes to mind.

Focus on the kind of person you wanted to BE, before writing about the things you wanted to DO.

Secondly, write down your obituary based on the life you are having right now and will continue to have based on your current experience.

Set aside some uninterrupted time to complete this exercise. You can re-visit this exercise again in the future, so do not try to perfect your answer now.

Questions you should ask yourself as you do this exercise are:

• What and/or who did you impact or change? Why?

• What character traits and values did you consistently demonstrate over your life? At your core, who were you?

• Who did you care for? How did you impact or change this person/these people?

• What were major accomplishments in your life? At the ages of 40, 50, 60, 70?

• What did you show interest in? What were you passionate or enthusiastic about?

• What was your legacy? The life you lead is the legacy you leave.

Based on what you have written, are there some life-changes you now want to make?

THINK BIG.

IMAGINE POSSIBILITIES.

RECALL INSPIRING DREAMS AND THOUGHTS YOU'VE HAD IN THE PAST.

Has this exercise helped move you closer to discovering or outworking your Life Purpose?

Appendix 2

Spiritual Gifts Questionnaire

With this questionnaire score yourself between 0 to 3, indicating to what extent the statement is true in your life. Do not look at or write on the 'score sheet' until after completing the questionnaire.

Much = 3, Some = 2, Little = 1, Not at all = 0

1. I often speak in ways that upset the traditions of people.
2. I enjoy taking responsibility for the well-being of people.
3. I could effectively teach my areas of interest to others.
4. I like to encourage the wavering, troubled or the discouraged.

5. I desire to manage money well in order to give liberally to worthy causes.
6. I enjoy assisting leaders and those in charge so that they can focus on their essential tasks.
7. I have a desire to work with the disadvantaged in order to help give them dignity and alleviate their suffering.
8. I like to persuade others to believe in what I think is important.
9. I would enjoy carrying the responsibility of leading a group of people to achieve an important purpose.
10. I enjoy breaking new ground with different ways of doing things.
11. When problems need to be resolved I tend to see the issues in terms of black or white and right or wrong.
12. I have enjoyed relating to the same group of people over a period of time, in their successes and failures.

13. I feel I can explain most things I know something about.
14. I feel I could help stir the complacent and encourage the discouraged to face their challenges.
15. I get a thrill out of giving things or money to initiatives I believe in.
16. I am satisfied just by knowing that my contribution has helped make an event go well.
17. I have felt an unusual compassion for those with physical, emotional or spiritual needs.
18. I can communicate in ways that are engaging and meaningful to the hearers.
19. I can organise ideas, people, resources and time for effective outcomes.
20. I feel I could begin in a pioneering situation and see new initiatives established.
21. Some people really appreciate my insights while others view me as a threat to the status quo.

22. I tend to know those I serve and guide intimately, and to be known well by them.
23. I enjoy devoting a lot of time researching and learning new material to communicate to others.
24. I find that people are often encouraged when I communicate with them and they feel a new lease of life.
25. I feel deeply challenged when confronted with urgent financial needs for causes I believe in.
26. I have enjoyed doing routine tasks that released others to be able to function effectively in what they do best.
27. I would enjoy visiting people in hospitals and/or retirement homes.
28. When I communicate I see a positive effect on the listeners.
29. I am a good judge of when to delegate responsibilities and to whom.

30. I find other people are excited and inspired to follow my vision.
31. If there is compromise within a group or hypocrisy, I am usually one of the first to discern it.
32. I have helped needy people by guiding them to words of hope and comfort.
33. I feel I can instruct others and see resulting changes in knowledge, attitudes, values and conduct.
34. I have inspired people to launch out in faith in an area.
35. I always like to give something if I meet beggars on the street.
36. I don't really mind when others get the credit for what I do.
37. I don't find it difficult to empathise with and help people who are hurting.
38. I enjoy sharing with people in order to bring about reconciliation and a greater sense of well-being.
39. When a leader shares his/her vision for a group to which I belong, I immediately start

thinking of all the things that need to be done in order to achieve the vision.

40. I have a strong desire to start projects in new areas.
41. I am able to perceive and warn against future dangers that most people are not even aware of.
42. I feel I am able to help restore people who have lost their way.
43. I like to equip and train people to be more effective in what they do.
44. I have comforted people in their difficulties in such a way that they felt helped and given fresh hope.
45. I live by the maxim that it is more blessed to give than to receive.
46. I don't need to be in the limelight but I like making everything run smoothly.
47. I would enjoy offering cheerful conversation to a lonely shut-in person, someone in prison, or somebody living on the streets.
48. I feel grieved when I see hopelessness in people and I feel

compelled to do something about it.

49. I am able to coordinate the activities of a group of people so that their different gifting complements each other and they function as a unified team.

50. I would enjoy being sent to start something that has never been done before.

Scoring Your Spiritual Gifts Questionnaire

Total your scores horizontally on the score sheet.

Place 1, 2, 3 up to 6 in the 'My Gifts' column of the highest scoring gifts. This will highlight your 'gift mix' combining both 'ministry' and 'motivational' gifts. The first three are your primary gifts. Gifts 4 to 6 are your secondary gifts.

Spiritual Gifts Score Sheet							
Value of Answers					Total	My Gifts	Key
1	11	21	31	41			P
2	12	22	32	42			S
3	13	23	33	43			T
4	14	24	34	44			E
5	15	25	35	45			G
6	16	26	36	46			H
7	17	27	37	47			M
8	18	28	38	48			E
9	19	29	39	49			L
10	20	30	40	50			A

Key:

P – Prophetic/Perceiver/Reformer/Non-conformist

S – Shepherd/Pastoral/Care-giver/ Guide/ Mentor/ Nurturer/Humaniser

T – Teaching/Instructor/Educator/Trainer/ Researcher

E – Exhortation/Encourager

G – Giving/Sharing/Contributor

H – Helping/Serving/Doing

M – Mercy/Compassion/Kindness

E – Evangelistic/Communicator/Networker /Recruiter/Reconciler

L – Leadership/Administration/Facilitation /Management

A – Apostolic/Visionary/Entrepreneurial/ Pioneer

Appendix 3
Identify Your Spheres of Influence

Identify those spheres of influence where you have a special concern or passion, and to which you gravitate.

The list below is not comprehensive so if your passion or area of calling is not listed, write in the space marked 'Other'.

Sphere/Domain

Education
- College/University
- Post-graduate
- Adult education
- Secondary/High School
- Pre-school

- Vocational
- Philosophy
- Curriculum
- Home-school
- Character development
-
-
-

Arts & Entertainment
- Art
- Music
- Dance
- Theatre
- Film/Movie
- Sports
- Architecture
- Comedy
- Literature
-
-
-

Health
- Public health
- Healthcare
- Mental/psychology

- Counseling
- Therapy
- Occupational
- Personal health
- Nutrition
- Animal health
-

Media

- Press/journalism
- National
- Local
- TV and radio
- Internet
-
-

Family

- Parenting
- Child development
- Marriage
- Elderly
- Extended family
- Widows
- Orphans
- Single parent
-
-

Economy & Business
- Public sector
- Private sector
- Employment
- Primary/raw materials
- Secondary/manufacturing
- Tertiary/services
- Management
- Sales/marketing
- Advertising
- Ethics
- Taxation
- Utilities
- Balance of trade/national debt
- Finance/banking
- Stock market
- Accounting
-
-

Science & Technology
- Environment
- Climate change
- Weather
- Biology/genetics
- Physics

- Chemistry
- Earth
- Biomedical
- Epidemiology
- Research
- Innovation
-
-

Government/politics

- International
- National
- Local
- Legislation/legal
- Judiciary/justice
- Executive
- Armed forces
- Prisons
-
-

Religion

- Church
- Mission agencies
- Bible schools
- Cross-cultural mission
- Other faiths
- Poor and needy

- Homeless
-
-

Social/non-profit
- Humanitarian
- Relief & development
- Charities
- NGO's
- Foundations
-
-

Infrastructure
- Planning
- Telecommunications
- Transportation
- Energy
- Waste management
-
-

Agriculture
- Land management
- Forestry
- Animal husbandry

- Organic farming
- Agricultural science
- Factory farming
- Free range
- Sustainable agriculture
- Urban agriculture
-
-

Other

-
-
-
-
-

People Groups

Age

- Infants
- Pre-schoolers
- Children
- Teens
- College/university students
- Career singles
- Young marrieds
- Couples

- Young parents
- Parents of teens
- Older people
- Other:

Cultural/geographic
- Extended family
- Neighbourhood
- City
- Nation
- Internationals/diaspora
- Region
- People group
- Muslim
- Buddhist
- Hindu
- Tribal
- Communist
- Jewish
- Women
- Men
- Other:

People needs
- Deaf
- Blind
- Disabled

- Special needs
- Homeless
- Poor
- Debt
- Unemployed
- Wealthy
- People of public influence
- Other:

7 Keys to Unlocking Your Life P.U.R.P.O.S.E.

Author

Stuart Simpson is the co-founder of Catalyst Ministries (*catalystmin.org*) and founder of Empower Coaching (*stuartmsimpson.com*).

Having lived and worked in five countries across three continents, he is currently based in the UK.

Through coaching and training, Stuart empowers people to discover their God-given design and live out their life purpose. He has a doctorate in ministry, with a specialisation in cross-cultural and kingdom mission.

He is the author of several books, including *7 Keys to Unlocking Your Life P.U.R.P.O.S.E.*, *Empowered! Discovering Your Place in God's Story*, *Kingdom Mission: A Call to Disciple Nations* (co-authored), and the *Personal Vision Journal/Notebook*.

7 Keys to Unlocking Your Life P.U.R.P.O.S.E.

Contact Details

If you would like further assistance or help with discovering your God-given design and/or unlocking your life purpose, please contact me.

Stuart Simpson
@
Web: www.stuartmsimpson.com

Email: empowercoach7@gmail.com

Instagram/Facebook/Twitter: empowercoach7

Personal Vision
Journal/Notebook

This Personal Vision Journal/Notebook has been designed especially for people with vision, dreamers, and for those who just want to make a positive difference in the world.

It is an ideal resource for those wishing to develop and record their own personal visions for their lives, which may become a blueprint for important life and career decisions.

Most of the book is ruled for you to make notes and jot down ideas. There is also blank space around the margins to doodle, sketch, stick pictures or do whatever you want! Use it in any way that seems helpful to you.

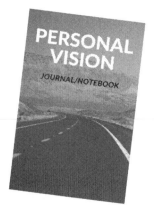

On every page there is a motivational quote...to inspire and motivate you to not only have vision, but to also pursue it and take the necessary steps to bring your visions to reality.

To also help with this, at different sections within the book, you are invited to think about your passions, your values, your goals, and making a Vision Board.

Available from Amazon or Empower Coaching at *www.stuartmsimpson.com*

Do You Feel *Disempowered* in Church?

Surveys indicate that most Christians feel disempowered. Wrong thinking separates the whole of life into 'spiritual' and 'secular', and creates a division within the Church between those in 'full-time' ministry and those who are not. This has robbed many believers of the joy of knowing their life can make a difference.

This book will:

- Challenge how you view the Great Commission and missions
- Sweep away old, disempowering mindsets that cause you to feel like a second-class citizen in the kingdom of God
- Show that YOU have a special God-given role and place in the fulfillment of God's story
- Help you practically discover your life passion and calling, and who God has made you to be
- Help you engage and live out your life-story within God's story and mission.

"A sweeping, cobweb-clearing vision"

– Larry Peabody, author of Serving Christ in the Workplace

"A thoroughly stimulating guide"

– Alan Hirsch, thought-leader & key mission strategist

"I love this book! The truths in this book will change the world!"

– Larry Kreider, Dove International Director

Do You Know Your Kingdom Calling?

Many Christians want their lives to make a kingdom difference. But in order to do so, most people have never taken the time to discover how God has made them. Consequently, life goes by without a clear sense of personal vision and life purpose.

If you want to gain that clarity so you can be intentional in making your best contribution to fulfilling God's kingdom purpose in and through your life, Stuart Simpson can help you.

Using a wholistic coaching model, Stuart helps people discover their God-given design and life purpose. He empowers believers and churches to engage in the full scope of the Great Commission, including the often overlooked mandate to disciple nations.

"Discover Your Purpose" Workshops & Course

"Empowered to Engage" Workshop

Other Coaching Tools

Personal Timeline
Wheel of Life Balance
Life Phases, Turning Points &
Convergence
LifePower Programme

Endnotes

Introduction
[1] Ephesians 4:12 states that leaders should equip the people for 'works of service'.
[2] Acts 9, Isaiah 6, Exodus 3.
[3] Matthew 25:14-30, Luke 19:12-27.

Chapter 1 – What is Life About?
[4] George Gaylord Simpson, 1967, *The Meaning of Evolution, revised edition.*
[5] https://www.theguardian.com/lifeandstyle/2012/sep/14/wasps-what-use-chris-packham.
[6] https://answersingenesis.org/what-is-the-meaning-of-life/humans-purposely-designed/.
[7] 1 Corinthians 9:26, New International Version.

Chapter 2 – Discovering Your Life Purpose
[8] Colossians 1:16, The Message Bible.
[9] A career is a subset of vocation, a line of work which will be a part of fulfiling one's calling. Careers can change during a lifetime and there may be several careers that fulfil any vocation.
[10] Rick Warren, *The Purpose-Driven Life: What on Earth Am I Here For?* (Zondervan Publishing), 2002), 21.
[11] https://www.quora.com/What-do-Buddhists-believe-the-purpose-of-life-is.
[12] Ephesians 2:10, New International Version.
[13] Psalm 145:13; Daniel 2:44, 4:3, 7:14, 27; Luke 1:33; Hebrews 1:8; Revelation 11:15.
[14] My unique Spiritual Gifts Questionnaire is included in the appendix of my book, *Empowered! Discovering Your Place in God's Story*.

Chapter 4 – Key #2 - Uniqueness
[15] This is the title of a book by John Mason.
[16] Reader's Digest article - https://www.rd.com/health/wellness/unique-body-parts/

http://www.bbc.com/future/story/20170109-the-seven-ways-you-are-totally-unique.
[17] Ephesians 2:10.

Chapter 7 – Key #5 - Origins
[18] https://www.firstthingsfirst.org/early-childhood-matters /brain-development/.
[19] Dr. Ronald W. Richardson, Family Ties that Bind (4th Ed.), 2011.
[20] Jeff Myers & David A. Noebel, *Understanding the Times: A Survey of Competing Worldviews*, 2018.

Chapter 8 – Key #6 – Skills & Abilities
[21] For more details, visit my Empower Coaching website at *www.stuartmsimpson.com* or *www.highlandsco.com*.
[22] Included in the appendix of my book, *Empowered! Discovering Your Place in God's Story*, 2013, 2019.
[23] These relate to the three major passages on spiritual gifts, Ephesians 4, Romans 12, and 1 Corinthians 12.
[24] This Spiritual Gifts Questionnaire incorporates some question ideas from the Modified Houts Questionnaire published by the Fuller Evangelistic Association and adapted by Barry Austin, as used in the Youth With A Mission Leadership Development Course compiled by Stephen Mayers, version 2006. However, in order to not limit the gifts solely to a church context, some questions have been adapted while others are new to incorporate the broader definitions.

Chapter 9 – Key #7 - Experiences
[25] Victor E. Frankl, in his classic book, *Man's Search for Meaning*, writes, 'Forces beyond your control can take away everything you possess except one thing, your freedom to choose how you will respond to the situation. You cannot control what happens to you in life, but you can always control what you will feel and do about what happens to you.

---

[26] Tony Stoltzfus, *The Calling Journey: Mapping the Stages of a Leader's Life Call*, 2010, 25.

Conclusion – Where Do I Go from Here?

[27] Philippians 3:12, Amplified Bible.

[28] Genesis 12:1.

[29] https://www.greatbigscaryworld.com/write-your-own-obituary/.

Printed in Poland
by Amazon Fulfillment
Poland Sp. z o.o., Wrocław